THE NEW
CREEPY CRAWLY
COLLECTION

SPIDERS

by Enid Fisher
Illustrated by Tony Gibbons

Gareth Stevens Publishing
MILWAUKEE

8292260

Contents

Getting to know
spiders

Some people squeal when they see a spider. But there's no need to be frightened. Most spiders just want to get away so they can weave a web and catch a tasty insect, not a human!

The house spider is just one of 34,000 species, or types, of spiders that live all over the world, except at the polar regions.

Spiders have survived on Earth a long time, too — experts believe for more than 300 million years.

Have you ever seen a spider enlarged under a microscope? Do they all look alike? How do they weave their webs?

Join us now on a spider safari, and find out all about these fascinating creatures. Most are good friends, but a few are dangerous. It's good to find out who's who!

On eight legs

Let's take a look at the spider's body. Both male and female spiders have two main body parts — the head and chest region, and the abdomen.

The female's abdomen is much larger than the male's. This is because she needs to carry eggs.

The spider's eight long legs make it a champion runner and a very good climber. Using special tufts of hair that allow them to grip smooth surfaces, spiders can even walk on ceilings without falling off.

Most spiders also have eight eyes — two facing forward, four looking upward, and two guarding the rear — so you cannot easily creep up on a spider from behind without being noticed!

The many-eyed spider is often near-sighted. But, by using its feelers, it can still tell where it is and if there's an insect nearby.

The feelers, or *palps*, look like two short legs at the front of its body.

Now look between the palps. Can you find the spider's jaws, which can crush a captured insect and poison it to death? The spider then sucks the liquid center of its meal straight into its mouth, eating greedily.

Spiders are master web-builders. If you look under a spider's abdomen, at the very back, you will see its *spinnerets*. The spider's silk comes out of these and is used to build webs.

Have you noticed we haven't mentioned bones? That's because the spider doesn't have any! Instead, it has an outer shell. The shell acts like a suit of armor that protects the spider's soft insides.

And, if you step on a spider accidentally, you won't find a red mess under your foot. A spider's blood is pale blue or green!

Web-weavers

Do you know the story about the Scottish king, Robert the Bruce, who found shelter in a cave on the eve of the Battle of Bannockburn, way back in 1314? He happened to see a spider trying to weave a web across the mouth of the cave, but failing again and again. Yet the spider kept on trying, until at last it succeeded. Its courage inspired the great king to do exactly the same in battle the next day — and he won!

Many spiders spin large, circular webs, known as "orb-webs," to catch flying insects, just like the one on these two pages.

You have probably seen orb-webs in the garden, in the trees and bushes, or in the house between ceilings and light fixtures. They seem to appear out of nowhere. For the spider, however, they involve a lot of hard work.

How does the spider begin its web? First, it chooses a point that will form the top of the web and spins a single thread. The spider then waits for a breeze to waft it to the next anchor-point. The spider continues to move from place to place in this way, spinning as it goes, until it has a frame for the web.

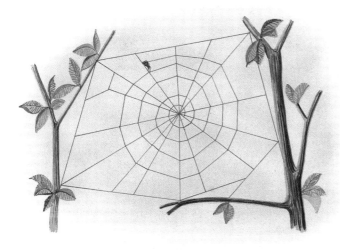

The spider now weaves "spokes" from the frame to a central point. Next, it spins silk around and around the spokes in bigger and bigger circles, until the pattern is finally complete.

The spider now sits still, waiting for its next meal to fly into the trap.

But not all webs are like this. The purse-web spider, for instance, lives in a silk tube, most of which is underground. The part above ground looks like the finger of a glove. The spider hides inside and drags passing insects through the walls of the web. Other spiders spin webs like funnels, which also lead to an underground lair. Here, the spiders wait to pounce on any unlucky insect that happens to step on the web.

Imagine following an insect that sees a lovely flower and flies straight toward the sweet scent. Suddenly, you realize it hasn't seen the spider's web in the way.

The hungry spider now creeps up from its hiding place at the edge of the web. It clamps its jaws around its prey and pumps in a jet of poison. Death comes quickly – the spider does not want to be kept waiting for its dinner!

Disaster! A horrible, sticky mess has trapped its wings. It fights and struggles; it kicks and wiggles; but it can't get free.

Now the spider quickly injects its dead prey with sticky juices from its mouth. The juices turn the insect's insides into a mush that the spider can easily suck.

the kill

Some spiders have terrible table manners! They spit out the hard bits, which they cannot digest, into their webs.

The spider will often eat what is left of its delicate-looking trap and begin to look for a new place to spin a web.

Most spiders can survive on one insect a day and will live happily on whatever passes by. Any insect unlucky enough to get caught will provide a nourishing meal for this mini-predator.

Webs must be replaced often because they are easily damaged by wind, rain, or even dew. Most garden spiders have to construct a new web every day in order to trap their next meal to survive.

Around

Many spiders live indoors. The house spider, for example, lives inside most of the time, especially in autumn and winter, setting up its household in warm, secluded corners.

the house

A house spider's life is sometimes dangerous, especially when humans get busy with vacuum cleaners and brooms!

House spiders are harmless. In fact, they are very useful creatures. They catch prey and try to keep out of your way as much as possible.

Without spiders, your home could be buzzing with undesirable insects.

Many different kinds of spiders probably live in your house or apartment. One of them is so tiny it can easily fit on your fingernail.

This tiny creature is the money spider. According to legend, if one crawls onto your hand, money is sure to come your way.

Never kill a spider. If you can't ignore it, try to trap it by gently sliding a sheet of stiff paper underneath it. Then quickly cover it with a clean, dry drinking glass before it has a chance to scurry away. Carry the spider outside as you hold the glass in place over the paper. Now you can set it free.

Most people think a spider that finds its way into the bathtub has made a heroic climb up the inside of the drainpipe and through the plug hole. But it can't — it would drown. So how did it get there? The most likely explanation is that it lost its footing on a nearby wall, or perhaps was wafted in on a breeze. Once dumped into the vast shiny "canyon" of your bathtub, however, there is no escape. Washing the spider down the drain does not set it free. It will drown long before it reaches the outdoors. Instead, try to save it in the way described above.

Underwater

Next time you pass near a pond of still water, do some detective work. See if there are any little splashes that seem to show something near the water's surface. You could be looking at evidence that a certain type of spider is alive and well and living in the pond!

These underwater spiders must come up for air from time to time, but they generally hide under water to ambush their prey.

Underwater spiders are also known as fishing spiders. They sometimes grab tiny fish and feast on them if they get too hungry while waiting for a passing insect.

spiders

This type of spider can't breathe in the water, so it has come up with a clever plan for storing an underwater air supply.

The underwater spider first spins its web, which lies flat just below the pond's surface. Then it swims up to the top and traps a bubble of air between its back legs, as shown in the picture on the opposite page.

Very carefully, it drags the bubble under the web by climbing down water plants. The spider may do this hundreds of times until the air has stretched the web into a kind of thimble shape.

Now the spider can live comfortably under water, waiting to trap insects for its daily meal.

The underwater spider also plans ahead. It provides itself with a special water thimble that holds enough air for about four to five months. This means it can nest under water for an entire winter season.

Fangs!

You've seen it in the movies. An enormous, scary-looking spider sinks its fangs into someone's skin. The pain is awful. The victim begins to sweat and feels very ill. But then a doctor arrives with a cure and saves him from serious illness, or even death.

Luckily, there aren't many spiders with poison strong enough to kill you. And, like some other animals, they usually don't attack first. It is very unlikely you will ever be bitten by one of these spiders in daily life. But you can't rely on a doctor being there if you *are* bitten, so you should be careful if you are in areas where these deadly species are commonly found.

All spiders have fangs, or jaws, that they use to bite their prey. Never annoy a spider, because some types may bite to protect themselves from you. That could be painful or, in rare cases, even fatal.

One spider that has been unjustly accused of being a killer is the tarantula. For some people, its name conjures up the image of a scary, furry monster waiting to strike with its deadly poison. The tarantula *is* large and furry, but its bite is about as dangerous as a bee's sting, so it is harmless to most humans.

The black widow spider is very dangerous, however. It earned its name because the female often feasts on the male after mating, as you can see in this picture. Its bite can kill, but it would actually prefer to run the other way. Keep away! Many black widows have bright red markings, but not all of them do.

18

business

Or you might carefully step onto the edge of her web and pluck a special rhythm on its strands, just like strumming a tune on a guitar. You might also catch an insect and wrap it up in your own silk. The female is so interested in her present that she allows you to come close without attacking.

After mating, however, you are in great danger. You still look like dinner to her! The black widow is known to eat her mate, and many other species try to do the same. What you must do is run for your life, ducking out from underneath her enormous body and scurrying away as quickly as possible.

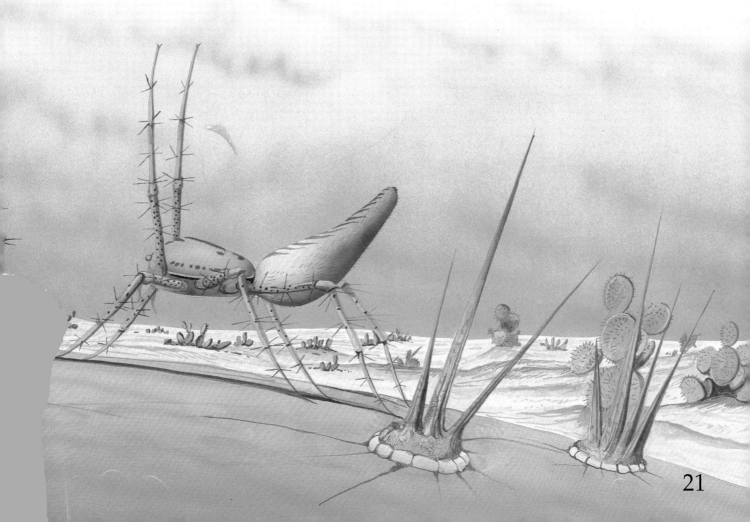

21

Did you know?

How long do spiders live?
Most outdoor spiders live only one season, but indoor spiders can live several years. A Mexican red-kneed spider has even been known to live for 28 years. It takes up to 12 years for some large spiders to become adults.

Which are the largest and smallest spiders?
The largest spider in the world is the Goliath spider, at 11 inches (28 cm) long with its legs outstretched. That's about as big as a dinner plate. The smallest is extremely tiny — no bigger than a bread crumb, in fact.

Is it true that some spiders can kill humans?
Some spiders can indeed kill. Their venom makes the victim shake, sweat, and vomit violently. Death sometimes follows. Luckily, scientists have developed cures for most of these spider bites.

▼ Do all spiders spin webs to catch their prey?
Not all spiders use webs to catch insects. Many hunt for food. Some, like the wolf spider, jump on their prey. The spitting spider spits out two lines of sticky glue that pin down the insect long enough for the spider to kill it. And the bolas spider, *below*, makes a ball of sticky thread at the end of a strand of silk and swings it at passing insects.

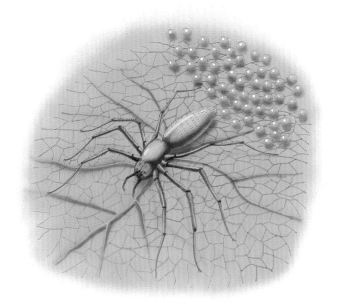

▲ How are spiders born?

The female (*above*) can lay up to 3,000 eggs, which she then wraps in a silk "blanket." This is attached to a plant or carried around on her back. When the spiderlings hatch, they stay in the "blanket," feeding off the egg yolks until they are big enough to catch their own food.

Do some peoples of the world really eat spiders?

Several native tribes around the world eat spiders that they know are not poisonous to ~~...~~ full of ~~...~~ But we do not recommend that you try eating spiders, in case you pick a poisonous one!

What is an arachnophobe?

An arachnophobe (A-RACK-NO-FOBE) is someone who is very frightened of spiders. (The scientific name for a spider is *arachnid*.) Arachnophobes cannot bear to be in the same room with even the smallest spider.

Do all spiders weave the same pattern?

All spiders of the same species weave the same pattern. But each species has its own special pattern that no other species can copy.

▼ Do all spiders live on insects?

While smaller spiders eat insects, some of the larger species can catch frogs, lizards, and even small birds.

23

Glossary

abdomen — the last, or posterior, section of a spider's body.

ambush — a surprise attack.

armor — a tough, protective covering.

camouflage — markings or coloring that help an animal or plant disguise itself and blend in with its natural environment.

fangs — long, pointed teeth that sometimes inject venom.

lair — the den or home of a wild animal.

orb — a circular form.

palps — sensory organs located near the mouth of spiders and insects.

predators — animals that hunt and kill other animals for food.

prey — animals that are killed for food by other animals.

secluded — hidden from view.

species — animals or plants that are closely related and often similar in behavior or appearance. Members of the same species are capable of breeding together.

spinnerets — the parts of a spider's body that produce the silk to spin webs.

tufts — short clusters of hairs.

venom — a poison produced by an animal.

Books and Videos

Fascinating World of Spiders. Maria A. Julivert (Barron)

Scary Spiders. Steve Parker (Raintree Steck-Vaughn)

Spider. Stephen Savage (Thomson Learning)

Spiders Near and Far. Jennifer Dewey (Dutton Children's Books)

The Tarantulas. Carl Green and William Sanford (Macmillan Children's Books)

Spiders in Perspective: Their Webs, Ways, and Worth. (Educational Images video)

Webs of Intrigue. (National Geographic Society video)

Index